Previous page: The Queen and the Duke of Edinburgh celebrated their ruby wedding anniversary on 20 November 1987. From a series of photographs taken by Tim Graham at Windsor Castle to mark the occasion.

This page: The Governor-General's residence was the scene of the official welcoming ceremony at the start of the Duke and Duchess of York's visit to the island of Mauritius in September 1987.

THE ROYAL YEAR 1988

Photographed by

TIM GRAHAM

GUILD PUBLISHING LONDON

A FAMILY HOLIDAY
IN MAJORCA

August 1987

The Spanish royal family were hosts to the Prince and Princess of Wales and their two young children for a short holiday in the sun at their royal palace in Palma on the island of Majorca. During the holiday the two royal families posed for photographers on the steps of the Marivent Palace.

Below from left to right: Infanta Christina, King Juan Carlos, Prince Charles, the Princess of Wales with Princes William and Henry, Infanta Elena, Queen Sophia and Infante Felipe, the heir to the Spanish throne.

The two young princes, and in particular two-year-old Prince Henry, stole the show during the photocall. Prince Henry is seen here in the arms of King Juan Carlos (above left) and (left) holding Queen Sophia's puppy, Bobby. Facing page: Prince Henry pointing out to his mother the different cameras wielded by over 60 photographers at the photocall.

HAPPY 87TH BIRTHDAY
MA'AM

4 August 1987

Accompanied by close members of her family the Queen Mother celebrated her birthday in customary fashion at Clarence House, her London home. Her legendary smile and warmth have made her famous throughout the world and, although in her late eighties, she is still carrying out a busy schedule of public engagements up and down the country.

The Queen Mother greeted the enthusiastic crowds from the balcony of Clarence House (right) and then came out to the gates to receive the bunches of flowers pressed on her by groups of small children, watched by her grandchildren, Viscount Linley and Lady Sarah Armstrong-Jones (left) and Prince Edward and the Prince of Wales with the Princess (right).

The Croft Original British Open
Horse Trials Championship
took place from 14–16 August
at Gatcombe Park, the
Gloucestershire home of the
Princess Royal and Captain
Mark Phillips. During the
weekend the Princess Royal
(facing page right) celebrated
her 37th birthday. Captain
Mark Phillips (above left)
masterminded the event and is
himself an expert rider and
former member of the British
Olympic three-day event team.
Their two children, Zara
(above) and Peter (left) enjoyed
themselves enormously as well
as lending a helping hand.
Among the large crowds
attending this popular event
were Prince and Princess
Michael of Kent (facing page
left) whose own home at Nether
Lypiatt is only a few miles from
Gatcombe Park.

Facing page and left: The Duchess of York, accompanied by her husband, presented prizes after polo at Smith's Lawn, Windsor Great Park, in September. During her childhood the Duchess of York's parents were a regular part of the polo scene at Smith's Lawn, home of the Guards Polo Club and England's smartest club. During matches she and her sister often played with younger members of the royal family. Below: The Duchess of York during a visit to the city of Sheffield on 14 September when she and the Duke visited the Royal Hallamshire Hospital and The Star newspaper before lunching at Sheffield Town Hall.

The day after celebrating his third birthday on 15 September Prince Henry attended Mrs Mynor's nursery school in Kensington for the first time. On his first morning he was accompanied to school by his proud parents and his elder brother, Prince William who had once been a pupil there himself. Below: School over, Prince Henry left for the return journey to Kensington Palace proudly clutching a pair of binoculars made at school.

A VISIT TO THE PARADISE
ISLAND OF MAURITIUS

26 September – 1 October 1987

*The Duke and Duchess of York paid an official visit to the
tropical island of Mauritius set amid the sparkling blue seas
of the Indian Ocean. The aim of the visit was to promote
British Week, part of the celebrations for the island's
Festival of the Sea. After the action-packed six days of the
official visit the royal couple remained on the island to
enjoy a quiet, romantic holiday by the edge of the ocean.*

*Facing page: The Duke and
Duchess of York disembarking
from the aircraft at the start of
their visit. Below: Inspecting the
guard of honour formed by the
island's Special Mobile Force at
Le Reduit, the Governor-
General's residence on the first
day of the visit. Overleaf: An
official banquet in the Duke and
Duchess's honour took place at
Le Reduit on the first evening
of the tour.*

Facing page: After church on Sunday morning the Duke and Duchess of York went on a walkabout outside the cathedral. During their visit to Mauritius they were enthusiastically greeted wherever they went. Left: The Duchess of York feeding a fruit bat at the Black River Wildlife Centre, a famous Mauritian nature reserve. Below: The royal couple during a visit to the Special Mobile Force at Vacoas.

Engagements on the island included a visit to the Pamplemousses Botanical Gardens (left) and the opening of the Duke and Duchess of York Cultural and Handicraft Centre at Quatre Cocos (below and facing page above).

Below: No visitor to Mauritius can help but notice the miles of waving sugar cane as sugar is still by far the largest industry on the island. On the last day of their official visit the royal couple went to the Britannia Sugar Estate, one of the island's many large sugar plantations. They are seen here leaving the estate in the manager's car on their way to an informal clifftop picnic lunch.

Facing page left: The Princess Royal is one of the busiest members of the royal family and these two events in the autumn of 1987 illustrate her wide-ranging interests. Above: Visiting the Jaeger store, Regent Street in London's West End on 21 October to attend a reception as President of the British Knitting and Clothing Export Council. Below: As Chancellor of London University presiding at the University's Presentation Ceremony on 2 December. Above right: On 14 October the Duchess of Gloucester, Patron of the Asthma Research Council, attended the Starlight Ball at the Hilton Hotel, London. Below right: The Duchess of York visited St Bartholomew's Hospital, London on 22 October to open Surgery House, a 'Home from Home' for parents of sick children.

This page: The Princess of Wales, Colonel-in-Chief of the Royal Hampshire Regiment, visited the city of Winchester on 23 October to watch the laying-up of the old colours of the regiment's 1st Battalion. She inspected a parade of men from the battalion and then watched a march-past through the city centre from the steps of the Guildhall. In honour of the occasion the Princess wore the regimental brooch presented to her when she visited the regiment in Berlin in 1985.

Facing page and above: Prince Edward's visit to Crickhowell in Wales on 26 October began a week of intense Duke of Edinburgh Award Scheme activity in Wales. The group of Gold Award participants from North-East Surrey were taking part in a 50-mile expedition in the Black Mountains as part of their Gold Award. Prince Edward, himself a Gold Award holder, is now also an International Trustee of the Scheme which operates worldwide in over 40 countries. Right: On 15 February Prince Edward arrived at the Palace Theatre in London's West End for his first day of work as a theatrical production assistant clutching a box of tea bags, a prerequisite of any office boy. The prince has been interested in the theatre for many years and he was excited about starting his new career with Andrew Lloyd Webber's Really Useful Company, whose current successes include Phantom of the Opera, Les Misérables and Starlight Express.

Right: The Princess of Wales at the first Festival of National Parks held on 20 September at Chatsworth Park in the Peak District. The aim of the festival was to increase public awareness of the ten National Parks in England and Wales. The packed programme of events in the superb setting of Chatsworth included such English pursuits as morris dancing, well-dressing, drystone walling and sheepdog trials. Facing page: With her usual stylish elegance the Princess of Wales delighted the waiting crowds by wearing a Tudor-style dress in crushed purple and black velvet and adorned with a crucifix when she arrived at Garrard, the Crown Jewellers, on 27 October for a gala evening in aid of Birthright, of which she is Patron.

WEST BERLIN
AND GERMANY

1–7 November 1987

Excitement at the Prince and Princess of Wales' visit was intense and large crowds turned out to see the royal couple wherever they went during the seven hectic days of receptions, trade fairs, visits to the ballet and the opera, fashion shows and numerous walkabouts.

Facing page: The Princess of Wales during the reception at the Schoeneberg Town Hall in Berlin. This page: The day in Cologne included a tour of the city's historic cathedral.

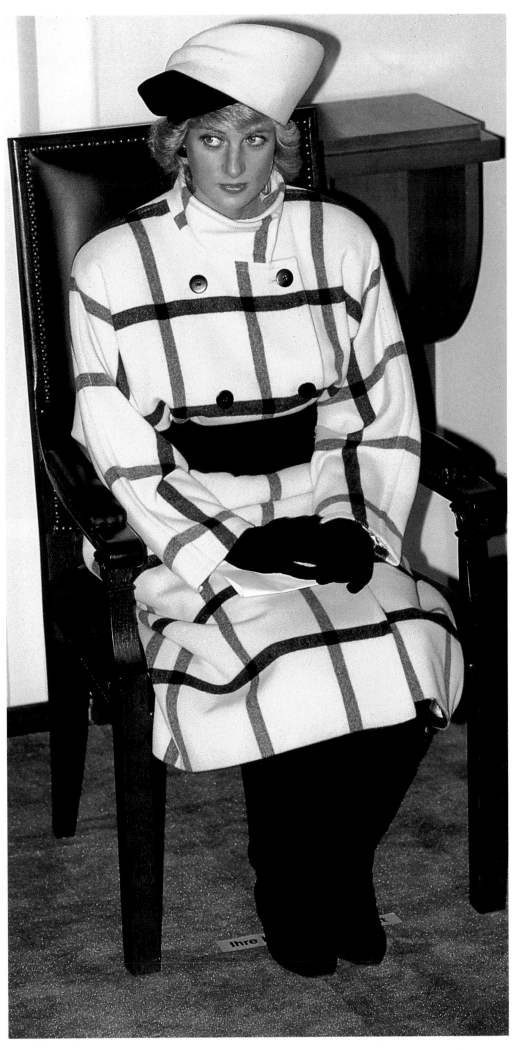

Above left: The Princess of Wales being greeted by rapturous crowds at Munich airport. Above right and right: At Bonn City Hall to sign the city's Golden Book, a ceremony they were to repeat many times during the next few days as every German town, even the smallest, has its Golden Book which is proudly brought out for signature by distinguished visitors. Facing page: For the dinner given in honour of the royal couple by the President of the Federal Republic the Princess of Wales treated fellow guests to a dazzling display of jewellery, including the diamond necklace, bracelet and earrings presented to her by the Sultan of Oman during their visit to his country in 1986.

For the Prince and Princess of Wales, who are both ardent opera lovers, one of the most enjoyable evenings of the tour was a visit to the Opera House in Munich to watch a performance of Mozart's Marriage of Figaro. *The Princess's dress of mauve and blue taffeta and velvet with a hem skimming her knees at the front and dipping to the floor at the back delighted the large crowd of 5,000 waiting outside the opera house.*

On 8 November members of the royal family, headed by the Queen (below right), attended the annual Remembrance Day Service at the Cenotaph in Whitehall and laid wreaths in honour of war victims and survivors. Left: Watching the service from a balcony were King Olav of Norway, the Princess of Wales, the Princess Royal, the Duchess of York and the Queen Mother. Right: The Prince of Wales in front of the Cenotaph flanked (right) by the Duke of Kent and (left) by the Duke of Edinburgh and the Duke of York.

On 12 November the Princess of Wales visted her former school, West Heath at Sevenoaks in Kent, to open the Rudge Sports Hall named in honour of the headmistress Miss Rudge who held the post for over 30 years until her retirement at the end of 1987. The Princess was accompanied by her two sisters, Sarah (Mrs Neil McCorquodale) and Jane (Mrs Robert Fellowes), and her lady-in-waiting, Miss Anne Beckwith-Smith who are all former pupils of the school. Left: Standing with the school's most famous old girl are Mrs Robert Fellowes, Miss Rudge and Mrs Neil McCorquodale.

The Queen and the Duke of
Edinburgh celebrated their ruby
wedding anniversary on 20
November. Their marriage at
Westminster Abbey in 1947 was
the first ceremonial occasion of
any splendour after the years of
war austerity, and the romance
between the shy, young Princess
who was the heir to the throne
and the tall, handsome Greek
prince who was also a British
naval officer had stirred the
public's imagination. The
Queen, who places much
emphasis on the importance of
family life, now delights in being
a grandmother. Tim Graham
was commissioned to take the
official photographs at Windsor
Castle to mark the occasion.

In November the Duchess of York completed a helicopter flying course at RAF Benson, a wedding present from Air Hanson. Determined to keep up with her husband whose love of flying is well known, she had already gained her fixed-wing pilot's licence in February and worked hard to gain her second licence, much to the admiration of other members of the royal family.

*Above left: Dressed as a red
goblin Prince Henry sets off to
take part in his nursery school's
nativity play on 9 December.
Above: The Queen leaving the
Deanery after attending
morning service at St George's
Chapel on Christmas Day.
Left: Christmas sees a large
family gathering at Windsor
Castle. Returning to the castle
after morning service on
Christmas Day are Princess
Michael of Kent with her
daughter Lady Gabriella
Windsor, the Princess of Wales
and Lady Davina Windsor, the
elder daughter of the Duke and
Duchess of Gloucester.*

After Christmas at Windsor Castle the Queen moves on to her private estate at Sandringham in Norfolk for six weeks of country life. During her annual stay a large succession of family and friends come to stay, including her four grandchildren who spent the New Year holiday at Sandringham. During the New Year photocall a beautifully maintained old estate fire engine kept the children amused while the Queen maintained a watchful eye. Prince William (right) was proud of his brightly polished brass helmet and (facing page below) Peter Phillips took control at the wheel.

AUSTRALIA'S BICENTENNIAL

25 January – 2 February 1988

The Prince and Princess of Wales went to Australia to take part in the celebrations surrounding the country's bicentennial. The visit was hot and exhausting but the royal couple's third visit to Australia was their most successful so far.

Facing page: The Princess of Wales disembarking from STS Young Endeavour, Britain's bicentennial present to Australia which Prince Charles had just handed over in a small ceremony. The ship is named after the English navigator and explorer Captain Cook's Endeavour. His was the first European ship to reach Australia in 1769 and Captain Cook then set about charting the east coast of the continent. The Young Endeavour had sailed from England with a joint crew of young Britons and Australians. Right: The Princess wore a succession of striking outfits on the tour, including this one of deep fuchsia pink, a favourite colour.

The Prince and Princess of
Wales arrived by barge to
officially launch the
Bicentennial Australia Day
Celebrations in front of Sydney
Opera House. After lunch they
watched a parade of 200 tall-
ships from the bridge of HMAS
Cook in the magnificent setting
of Sydney Harbour. Above: The
following day, after a short
flight to Melbourne, the Prince
and Princess attended a
Multicultural Festival.

To the strains of Glen Miller's
'In the Mood', the Prince and
Princess of Wales lead the
dancing at a bicentennial
dinner-dance in Melbourne. For
two minutes they danced alone
on the floor, Prince Charles
leading his wife at such a pace
until she breathlessly implored
him to slow down.

Above left: Temperatures of 103 degrees greeted the Prince and Princess on their visit to Goolwa near Adelaide but the Princess defied the sun by not wearing a hat. Above: Returning to Sydney on 30 January the Princess watched her husband open the Illawarra International Performing Arts Centre at Wollongong. Left: Attending a Bicentennial Service for Members of the Order of Australia at St Andrew's Cathedral in Sydney.

Above: At the Central Coast
Surf Carnival at Terrigal Beach
north of Sydney the Prince and
Princess of Wales drove along
the beach in a Land Rover.
Facing page: Later in the
afternoon the Princess presented
prizes to the winning team of
bronzed lifeguards. Much to her
amusement the 5-foot 10-inch
Princess discovered that she was
taller than these strong surfers
whose job it is to save hundreds
of lives each year. Right: The
Princess visiting Barnardo's Roy
McCaughey Welfare Centre at
Auburn near Sydney on the last
morning of their visit to New
South Wales. The Princess was
delighted to be in the company
of children again and had
confessed several times during
the tour that she was missing her
two young boys dreadfully.

A VISIT TO THE ANCIENT KINGDOM OF THAILAND

3 – 5 February 1988

After their successful visit to Australia the Prince and Princess of Wales travelled on to Thailand in South East Asia for a three-day visit marking the 60th birthday celebrations of King Bhumibol Adulyadej who has reigned since 1946.

On the first full day of the visit the Prince and Princess were taken on a tour of the Grand Palace and the Temple of the Emerald Buddha, two of Thailand's best known tourist attractions. The Grand Palace is no longer the King's residence in Bangkok but the Buddhist temple with its demon sentries guarding the entrance is the holiest place in Thailand and still serves as the King's private chapel.

Facing page: Arriving in Bangkok from Australia the Princess was delighted by the huge Thai parasols carried to protect her from the heat even though it was officially the cool season. Right: A river cruise along the Chao Phraya river to see the sights of Bangkok included lunch on board and a chance to enjoy some cool breezes. Below: In Chiang Mai, Thailand's northernmost city, the Princess visited the Bosang Umbrella Factory to see the famous painted bamboo umbrellas which are exported worldwide.

THE YORKS IN LOS ANGELES

26 February – 6 March 1988

The Duke and Duchess of York went to Los Angeles as Patrons of the three-month long UK/LA 88 Festival. The Californians loved the Duchess's cheery spirit which never flagged despite her pregnancy and the pouring rain and high winds which played havoc with her hats.

Right: Arriving at Los Angeles International Airport before driving to HMY Britannia, which was to be their base during the visit. Below and facing page: The Duke and Duchess of York in Chinatown to watch the celebrations for the Year of the Dragon.

Right: The Duchess of York at St Luke's Episcopal Church for the Sunday morning service. Below left: Opening the Asprey exhibition at Bullocks Wilshire store, one of several engagements to promote British trade during their visit. Below right: Arriving at the reception given in the royal couple's honour by the British consul-general. Facing page: The Duchess of York wore a stunning red and black outfit for the UK/LA 88 Gala Dinner at the Biltmore Hotel.

Left and facing page above:
Visiting the Retrospective
Exhibition of David Hockney's
Work at the Los Angeles County
Museum of Art, the Duke and
Duchess were escorted by the
British-born artist himself.
There was much laughter when
the Duchess read David
Hockney's inscription inside
their catalogue and pointed out
there was no 'T' in Duchess.
Facing page below: The Duke
and Duchess of York with Miss
Jean Muir at a glittering fashion
show of her clothes.

Right: The Duchess's hair
accessories were a talking point
of the trip. She sported LA hat
pins for the first day of
engagements, roses and a
hummingbird in her hair for the
Jean Muir Fashion Show and
flew the flag when she wore
three diamanté badges, two
Union Jacks and one Stars and
Stripes, to visit the David
Hockney Exhibition.

For the Duke of York the highlight of the visit to Los Angeles was a trip on board the USS Nimitz, the world's largest aircraft carrier. USS Nimitz took them on a three-hour trip out to sea to watch air operations from the deck of the carrier.

The Duke of York took part
in a 'slingshot' take-off in an
aircraft, travelling at 160 miles
per hour from the deck of the
carrier. The Duchess watched
wistfully, wishing that she could
have done it too but the closest
she came to flying on this
occasion was trying on the
Nimitz flying jacket and cap.

The last day of their visit to Los Angeles was spent on the UCLA campus where they were greeted by a boisterous crowd of enthusiastic students. The Duchess's duties on the campus included (above) touring the neonatal intensive care unit and paediatric ward during which she was subjected to a fair amount of teasing about her impending motherhood.

Right: Princess Margaret attending 'The Night of 100 Stars' on 20 March at the Adelphi Theatre in aid of Sunshine Homes and Schools for Blind Children of which she is President. Below left: Princess Michael of Kent at the Hotel Inter-Continental, London on 23 March when she and her husband were the guests of honour at the Spring Ball held in aid of The Westminster Society for Mentally Handicapped Children and Adults and PHAB. Below right: On 25 March the Duchess of Kent carried out engagements in St Albans, Hertfordshire with her husband the Duke of Kent, including opening the Lawn Tennis Association's Batchwood Indoor Tennis Centre. Facing page: The Princess of Wales meeting dancers backstage at the Sadler's Wells Theatre on 22 March when she attended a Gala Performance given by the London City Ballet of which she is Patron. One of the Princess's greatest interests is dancing and she makes time in her busy schedule to pay private visits to the company's ballet rehearsals.

Below and facing page: The Queen and the Duke of Edinburgh outside Lichfield Cathedral, Staffordshire after the traditional Maundy Thursday Service on 31 March. The Queen was attended by children of the Royal Almonry carrying traditional nosegays of sweet herbs and by the Queen's Bodyguard of the Yeomen of the Guard who play an important ceremonial part in the service. Maundy Service, dating back to the twelfth century, commemorates Jesus washing the feet of his disciples on the eve of the Crucifixion. Although the tradition of the monarch washing the feet of some of his poorer subjects was discontinued in the eighteenth century, the service still continues the tradition of distribution of alms or Royal Maundy to the poor.

Right: The Duchess of York at Olympia on 28 March to open the London Book Fair. For several years, both before and since her marriage to the Duke of York, the Duchess worked in London for a Swiss publisher specializing in fine art books.

On 6 April the Princess Royal (facing page) visited the Outward Bound Wales Centre at Aberdovey, a picturesque village on the mid-Wales coast to name the centre's new cutter The Marine Society. As it was the school holidays she brought along her ten-year-old son Peter Phillips who successfully tackled the assault course in true family tradition with grit and determination. He was also taught how to handle an inshore rescue boat belonging to the local lifeboat station.

STATE VISIT OF THE KING OF NORWAY

12–15 April 1988

King Olav V of Norway paid his second State Visit to Britain in April. His arrival was a colourful event, with all the splendid pageantry associated with British ceremonial occasions. Born in 1903, King Olav's mother was Princess Maud, one of Edward VII's daughters, and as well as being a close cousin of the Queen he is also a very good friend of the royal family and visits Britain frequently.

Facing page and above: After the welcoming ceremony in the Home Park, the Queen and King Olav drove in a carriage procession through the streets of Windsor to the castle, accompanied by a Sovereign's Escort of Household Cavalry, marching bands and colourful guardsmen. Left: The Princess Royal and Captain Mark Phillips were guests at the traditional Lord Mayor's Banquet held in King Olav's honour at the Guildhall in the City of London on the second evening of his State Visit.

This page: On 19 April the Duchess of Kent spent a day carrying out engagements in the county of Kent. Towards the end of the afternoon she paid a private visit to the Kent and Sussex Hospital in Tunbridge Wells to see the newly opened children's ward. The Duchess's never-failing smile and bedside manner delighted the children. Facing page: The Princess of Wales visiting St Albans, Hertfordshire on 14 April to open the new Maltings Shopping Centre.

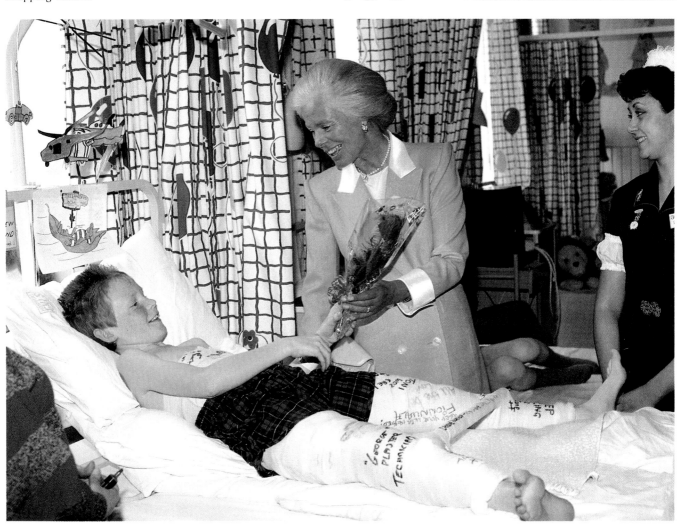

Below: On 25 April the Princess Royal launched Save the Children Week by officially opening the new British Rail Thameslink line to Blackfriars Station. Right: She then named a special train 'The Save The Children Week Special'.
Facing page: The Princess of Wales leaving Frinton-on-Sea, Essex on 26 April where she visited the homes of the Essex Voluntary Association for the Blind. The royal family travel frequently to engagements up and down the country in the distinctive red helicopters of the Queen's Flight, and for the Princess an added bonus of travel by helicopter is that she can usually be back home with her children in good time before they go to bed.

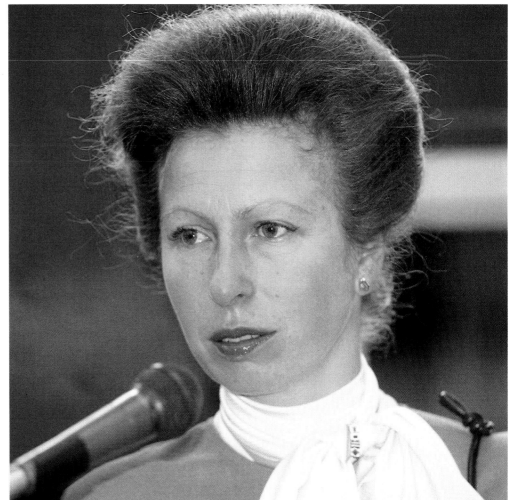

On 29 April the Prince and Princess of Wales visited Glasgow in Scotland to open the city's £50 million Garden Festival at Prince's Dock and to lay the Foundation Stone at the new Cathedral Halls and Visitor's Centre at Glasgow Cathedral. Yachts sounding their foghorns on the river Clyde, choirs, a jazz band and thousands of cheering onlookers gave the royal couple, Chief Patrons of the Festival, an enthusiastic welcome as they arrived at the 120-acre site. The Princess of Wales was wearing a striking mansize overcoat in royal blue, complete with collar and tie. After the opening ceremony the Prince and Princess toured the site in an open flower-bedecked train.

On 3 May the Princess of Wales, Patron of the British Red Cross Youth, named a British Rail 125 locomotive 'The Red Cross' at Paddington Station, London. The event was part of the celebrations marking the 125th anniversary of the founding of the Red Cross organization, now the world's largest charity. After the naming ceremony the Princess faced a three-foot drop from the locomotive cab (left) before going on to meet a group of handicapped young people with their Red Cross helpers (below).

*The start of the English polo
playing season saw the Prince of
Wales playing at Smith's Lawn,
Windsor Great Park on 2 May
for the Windsor Park team.
Prince Charles spends as many
summer afternoons on the polo
field as his busy schedule
permits.*

*Above and left: The Princess of
Wales brought Prince William
to watch his father play his first
match of the season and
together between matches they
helped other spectators stamp in
the divots torn up by the ponies'
hooves to keep the ground in
good condition. Watching polo
is an informal occasion much
enjoyed by the royal family and
the Princess underlined this
informality at the start of the
new season by wearing a jaunty
baseball cap, jeans tucked into
calf-length boots and a British
Lung Foundation sweatshirt.*

Left: Polo is a fast and exciting game to watch and there are frequent collisions at high speed between players. During his first match of the season on 2 May Prince Charles clashed sticks with an opponent who is seen here waiting for the St John's Ambulance team to arrive, having suffered a broken arm.
Below: During summer weekends at Windsor Castle the Princess of Wales often brings the young princes to watch their father play and to enjoy the company of other small children.

Facing page: A blooming Duchess of York in Hereford on 9 May to open the new headquarters of the Herefordshire Federation of Young Farmers' Clubs.

The Royal Windsor Horse Show is held each year in mid-May. With Windsor Castle and the river Thames as a backdrop it is a picturesque event in the English summer calendar and popular with the royal family. As well as top-class show-jumping, dressage and other ring events in the Home Park, the show includes international driving, a sport at which the Duke of Edinburgh excels. Although the Queen and the Duke of Edinburgh had only returned from their bicentennial tour of Australia a few days before this year's show, Prince Philip competed in the driving competition which takes place over three days. On the first day which covers dressage and presentation the Queen put in a brief appearance to watch Prince Philip (facing page) put a team of her black fell ponies through their paces.

Left: The Duchess of York visited the Royal Windsor Horse Show to watch her father, Major Ronald Ferguson take part in the judging of heavyweight polo ponies and (below) presented rosettes to a winning pony club team. Facing page above: The most arduous part of a three-day driving event is the marathon on the second day when the skills of the ponies and their driver are fully tested. Prince Philip setting off in style along the Long Walk and (below) going through one of the obstacles on the marathon course.

For the Royal Windsor Horse Show the Queen (facing page) has a full houseparty at Windsor Castle and this year's gathering included (left) Prince Edward enjoying an informal ride around the Great Park. Below left: The Duke of York on leave from his ship HMS Edinburgh and Prince Edward with Mr Roland Wiseman, the Deputy Ranger. Below right: The Queen and Princess Margaret watching the marathon driving event in Windsor Great Park.

Right: The Queen descending the cathedral steps after a service of the Order of the British Empire at St Paul's Cathedral on 17 May. Below: Leaving St Paul's Cathedral with the Duke of Edinburgh, Grand Master of the Order.

Facing page: Proudly clutching two paintings Prince Henry leaves nursery school with his nanny on his first day back after a nine-day absence following a minor operation.

Facing page: On 20 May the Queen and the Duke of Edinburgh visited Peterborough to attend a service at the city's cathedral on the occasion of its 450th anniversary.

This page: Princess Alexandra, as Patron of the Leeds Castle Foundation in Kent, visited the castle with her husband, the Hon. Angus Ogilvy, on 25 May to open the redesigned Golf Course, Aviary, Maze and Grotto.

This page: The Princess Royal with her children, Zara and Peter Phillips, at the Windsor Three-Day Event which took place between 27 and 29 May in Windsor Great Park. Left: The Princess Royal, President of the Event, received a giant cheque for Save the Children Fund of which she is President.
Facing page: On 4 June the Princess Royal, accompanied by her daughter Zara, went to Cirencester Park, the Earl of Bathurst's 3000-acre estate in Gloucestershire, to watch Prince Charles play polo in the semi-finals of the Committee Cup.

Derby Day, which took place this year on 1 June, is part of Britain's colourful tradition and a great day out for many Londoners as well as being a grand social occasion. Both the Queen and the Queen Mother are successful racehorse owners and the Queen usually takes a large party to Epsom Racecourse to watch the Derby, the most famous horserace in the world. This year the royal party included (left) the Queen Mother, (right) the Duchess of Gloucester, and (far right) Prince Philip and the Princess Royal. Below: Watching the crowds from the royal box are Princess Michael of Kent, the Princess Royal, the Queen and the Queen Mother. Overleaf: Prince and Princess Michael of Kent with the Queen.

Facing page: The Duchess of York at Smith's Lawn, Windsor Great Park on 8 June when she presented prizes for the Reebok Trophy in aid of Cancer Research. Below: One of the prizewinners was the Duchess of York's brother-in-law, the Prince of Wales, who won a trophy for polo.
Right: On 5 June the Queen presented the prizes at the finals of the Queen's Cup, the most prestigious tournament in the English polo season which takes place at Smith's Lawn, Windsor Great Park.

*Above: The Queen leaving
Buckingham Palace on her way
to Horse Guards Parade in
Whitehall for the ceremony of
Trooping the Colour on 11
June. The colourful ceremony to
mark the monarch's official
birthday began in 1755 in
the reign of George II and
during the present Queen's reign
has taken place on the second
Saturday of June. Below: Prince
William on his way to Horse
Guards Parade to watch the
ceremony.*

After Trooping the Colour is over the royal family return to Buckingham Palace to watch the Queen's procession return down the Mall. Watching from the Palace balcony were (left) the Princess of Wales holding Prince Henry in her arms and in front Lady Rose and Lady Davina Windsor, the daughters of the Duke and Duchess of Gloucester. Below from left to right: Princess Margaret, the Princess of Wales with Prince Henry and Lady Rose and Lady Davina Windsor in front, and Prince and Princess Michael of Kent with their children, Lord Frederick Windsor and Lady Gabriella Windsor.

The Garter Day Ceremony is one of the oldest English traditions and takes place at Windsor Castle at the beginning of Royal Ascot Week in the middle of June. The Queen (facing page) is Head of the Order which was founded by Edward III in 1348 and is dedicated to St George, the patron saint of England. The procession from Windsor Castle to St George's Chapel for the annual Service is a magnificent scene of pageantry with marching bands and colourful footmen and men of the Household Cavalry lining the route. The Prince of Wales (left) is by tradition one of the twenty-four Knights of the Garter whose appointment is the sovereign's choice alone. The distinctive dress, including black velvet hats with ostrich plumes, has remained unchanged since the seventeenth century. The first Tudor king, Henry VII, added the Collar or gold chain with its Tudor roses and pendant badge of St George to the dress.

The four-day Royal Meeting at Ascot in June is the highlight of the English summer season, both as a sporting occasion and as a social one with the ladies' elegant fashions attracting almost as much attention as the famous thoroughbred horses. *Facing page above:* The Queen and Prince Philip lead the procession of open landaus bringing the royal party from nearby Windsor Castle half-an-hour before the start of each afternoon's racing. *Left:* The Princess of Wales in a distinctive black-and-white spotted dress makes her way through the crowds. *Above:* The Queen Mother, accompanied on Ladies Day by the Princess of Wales in elegant dove-grey, always receives an enthusiastic welcome from the crowds lining the railings as the landaus drive down the course to the Royal Enclosure. *Right:* The Princess of Wales escorted by the Duke of Westminster.

Above: The Duchess of York and Princess Margaret arriving at Royal Ascot on Ladies Day and (below) Princess Margaret on her way to view the horses. Facing page: The Duchess of York, then seven months pregnant, wore bright yellow accompanied by a large black straw hat on the opening day of Royal Ascot.

This year's Rolex Celebrity Challenge clay-pigeon shoot to raise money for the SEARCH '88 Cancer Trust took place at the famous Gleneagles Hotel on 26 June and brought together a varied cast of celebrities from the worlds of royalty, aristocracy, sport and entertainment. Left: The Princess Royal came along to watch her husband Mark Phillips shoot for The Team which included (facing page above) the Duke of Kent and (below) Prince Edward, seen here seated between Jackie Stewart, the former world champion racing driver who organizes the annual event, and Captain Mark Phillips.

A romantic train ride from Victoria Station, London to Vienna on board the Orient Express was how Prince and Princess Michael of Kent celebrated their tenth wedding anniversary at the end of June. The royal couple were delighted to be returning to Vienna where they had been married and were accompanied on the journey by their nine-year-old son, Lord Frederick Windsor. For the charity trip which raised over £50,000 in aid of the Thames Valley Hospice in Oxford, the Prince and Princess were the guests of the Orient Express's owners, Mr and Mrs James Sherwood.

Facing page above and far left: The Princess of Wales at Smith's Lawn, Windsor Great Park on 29 June to watch polo sponsored that afternoon by the magazine Holà in aid of the National Hospital for Nervous Diseases, London of which she is Patron. Left: The Duchess of York arriving at Smith's Lawn, Windsor Great Park on 10 July with her puppy Bendicks. She had come to present polo prizes in aid of the Anastasia Trust for the Deaf of which she is Patron.

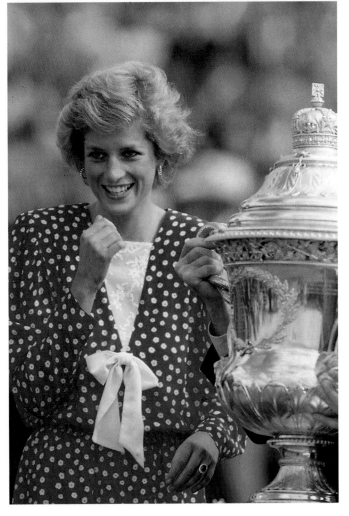

Above: The Princess of Wales arriving at Smith's Lawn, Windsor Great Park on 13 July to watch polo in aid of the British Lung Foundation of which she is Patron. Left: Cartier International Polo on 24 July was a much sunnier occasion and the Princess of Wales presented the beautiful Coronation Cup to the winning team, England who beat North America in a close match by eight goals to seven.

The President of Turkey paid a State Visit to Britain for four days in mid-July. On the third night of his visit he hosted a banquet at Claridge's Hotel which many members of the Royal Family attended. Facing page: The Princess of Wales arriving at Claridge's wearing a striking aquamarine evening dress with the Family Order, a miniature of the Queen, pinned on one shoulder. Right: The Duchess of Gloucester (left) talking to the Duchess of Kent as the Royal Family assembled at Claridge's. Below: The Duchess of Kent in full evening dress, including a magnificent tiara.

In July celebrations were held up and down the country to commemorate the tercentenary of the monarchs William and Mary and the Glorious Revolution. Prince William of Orange had arrived at Torbay from the Netherlands in July 1688 and the Queen and Prince Philip, accompanied by the present Prince of Orange, the heir to the Dutch throne, visited the West Country to carry out a series of engagements to commemorate the historic event. Below: The Queen arriving in Torquay on 20 July. She and Prince Philip then embarked on HM Yacht Britannia (facing page above). Right: After visiting Torbay the Queen went on to Plymouth on 22 July to carry out a series of engagements.

Facing page below: A regular fixture in the royal calendar is the Royal Tournament held each July at Earl's Court, London. On 28 July the Prince and Princess of Wales attended accompanied by their two sons, Prince William and Prince Henry.

The 'Wedding of the Year' took place on 30 July at Saffron Walden in Essex between Mr James Ogilvy, the son of Princess Alexandra and the Hon. Angus Ogilvy, and Miss Julia Rawlinson. Right: The Queen arriving at the church for her godson's wedding with Princess Alexandra and the Hon. Angus Ogilvy. Below left: The Princess of Wales and Princess Margaret dressed in summer silks for the wedding. Below right: Princess Michael of Kent arriving with her son, Lord Frederick Windsor.

Facing page: The newly married couple pose for photographers with their four bridesmaids. From left to right: Miss Charlotte Rawlinson, Lady Gabriella Windsor, daughter of Prince and Princess Michael of Kent, Alexandra Wilson and Miss Eleanor Rawlinson.

*The highlight of the royal year
was the birth of a daughter to
the Duke and Duchess of York.
The newest Princess who
weighed 6 pounds 12 ounces
was born at 8.18 p.m. on the
eighth day of the eighth month
of 1988. The birth took place
at the Portland Hospital in
London with the Duke of York
in attendance. The Princess of
York is fifth in line to the throne.*

This edition published 1988 by
Guild Publishing
by arrangement with
Michael O'Mara Books Limited, London
and Independent Television News Limited

CN 6101

Copyright © 1988 by Tim Graham

Typeset by Florencetype Ltd, Kewstoke, Avon
Printed and bound by Printer Industria Grafica SA, Barcelona, Spain